Managing Communication

Managing Communication

Puneet Srivastava

Rupa . Co

Published 2005 by

Rupa . Co

7/16, Ansari Road, Daryaganj,
New Delhi 110 002

Sales Centres:

Allahabad Bangalore Chandigarh Chennai
Hyderabad Jaipur Kathmandu
Kolkata Mumbai Pune

Typeset in 12 pts. Times Roman by
Nikita Overseas Pvt. Ltd.
1410 Chiranjiv Tower
43 Nehru Place
New Delhi 110 019

Printed in India by
Saurabh Printers Pvt. Ltd.
A-16, Sector IV
Noida 201 301

Contents

Preface

'IT SEEMS, there has been a communication gap!'

This is a sentence we use so often. This volume is a simple effort to help readers avoid using it, at least on some occasions.

This book covers some practical tips for effective communication in formal and professional set-ups. Further, communication is a two-way process, and accordingly this book addresses the needs over both the fronts.

Students and youngsters would find the book especially useful in harnessing their communication skills to match the needs and requirements of coming times.

My gratitude to beloved Guruji, Sri G. Narayana, for sharing his wonderful stories with us and allowing us to share them with others.

Introduction

WHENEVER SOMEONE asks the question – What's Communication? I am instantly reminded of the famous story from the *Mahabharata*.

During the battle of Kurukshetra, when the Pandavas were not able to get past Dronacharya, the chief of the Kaurava army, Krishna came up with a plan.

He said, let's give Dronacharya the false news of the death of his son, Ashwathama. Krishna knew that this news would be powerful enough to distract Drona's attention and gain an opportunity to defeat him.

Next day, when the battle was in full swing, as per the plan, Bhima killed an elephant named Ashwathama and arranged for the news of Ashwathama's death to reach Dronacharya.

Dronacharya was a clever man, conversant in all the ways of the war. When he came to know of the death, he said that he wouldn't believe a word unless someone as truthful as Yudhisthir would confirm it.

Yudhisthir, who was known to speak only the truth, came up and said, 'Ashwathama killed; but not the man, the elephant.'

However, the moment Yudhisthir had finished saying 'Ashwathama killed', Krishna blew a conch-shell *(shankh)* and other Pandava warriors joined him in creating a commotion, causing the latter part of the sentence to be drowned in the noise. Thus, Dronacharaya could only get to hear 'Ashwathama killed'!

Now that's what I call Communication!

What you say is important, but what is more important is:

- How it's presented
- What gets received
- How it's interpreted

Further, communication can take place through countless number of channels and for an infinite number of reasons. Thus, communication could be a casual chat between two friends; but communication could also refer to some document as important as the Constitution of the country.

It is not possible to cover the entire spectrum of communication modes in a slim volume. Nor is this necessary. Our focus in this book will be on Inter-personal Formal Communication, both written and verbal.

We will discuss certain tips that should help you communicate more effectively, primarily at your work/professional front.

Our discussion will cover the following forms of outgoing and incoming communications:

Now that's ... Communication!

Section A – Written Communication

- Writing Letters
- Writing E-mails
- Reading

Section B – Verbal Communication

- Public Speaking
- Presentations
- Meetings, Interviews and Negotiations

SECTION A
WRITTEN COMMUNICATION

*

Writing Letters

*

MOBILE PHONES and Internet might be the 'in-things', our preference might be shifting towards E-mail and SMS, nevertheless the good old letter, written or typed on a sheet of paper, still remains the principal mode of formal and official communication.

Unfortunately, with the advent of new technology based tools our letter writing skills seem to have taken a serious beating, and many of us face genuine difficulties in composing formal letters.

In this chapter, we will discuss some tips to effective letter writing for professional and general purposes.

The readers may please take note that this book does not cover 'letter writing' from the examination point of view. It is advised to refer to some prescribed book of English grammar for this purpose.

The process of writing a professional letter has to be understood at two levels:

1. Conceptual Level
2. Practical Level

Conceptual Level – Letter Writing

At the time of writing a letter, we need to keep three questions in the mind:

- Who are we writing to?
- What are we writing for?
- What do we expect in return?

Let's discuss each in detail...

Who are we writing to?

This question is important because it helps us choose the right tone for the letter. By tone we mean the manner of expression. Let's understand it further with the help of an analogy.

Suppose we are responding to a job advertisement in the newspaper and are writing a covering letter for our CV or Bio-Data. Let's see how the tone of the letter could vary, depending on whom the letter is being addressed to. Three possible scenarios are discussed here.

1. If the application were to be addressed to the CEO or someone similar, it means, this appointment might be of significant strategic importance to the organisation and

selection might be taking place under the direct supervision of the decision-maker. Hence, what we write in our letter might just work out to be even more important than our CV, at least for the initial rounds of scrutiny. Thus, highlighting our USP (Unique Selling Proposition) and our suitability for the job in distinct terms attains significance in this case. In such a scenario we could adopt a direct and assertive tone for our letter.

2. If the letter is being sent to the HR Department in general, then it is most likely to be read by one of the executives as a matter of routine. She/He would match our qualifications and experience with the given set of criteria, and would accept or reject our candidature for the next round of scrutiny. Hence, we need not be too assertive in writing such an application. We should do well by providing sufficient information to prove that we are suitable for the job. Our letter in this case should more or less balance our CV.
3. If we happen to be replying to a P.O. Box address, where the identity of the advertiser has not been disclosed, our letter could simply be a courtesy cover letter accompanying the CV and hope that our CV will eventually do the rest of the talking.

Similarly, suppose we are writing a Sales Promotion letter. In this case also our tone would vary, depending on if:

1. We are writing to the customer (decision maker) directly
2. We are writing to some representative of the customer, say a Manager, etc.
3. We are writing to a channel partner or an agent, who would re-sell the proposal to the end customer

The general rule is: *Imagine yourself in the shoes of the expected reader and ask – What kind of a letter would make him/her take a decision in my favour?*

Please remember, you don't need to go overboard in expressing yourself on every occasion. You will have to use your discretion and your judgement in deciding what kind of a tone would be appropriate for the occasion on a case-to-case basis.

What are we writing for?

Unpacking this question would give us:

- Why am I writing this letter?
- What message do I want to convey through this letter?

Continuing with our analogy of a job application, a possible objective of writing the job application could be – *'to be called for an interview'*.

Knowing this objective should immediately provoke us to ask:

- What would ensure that I get called for the interview?
- What would make the reader shortlist my CV out of the thousands of applications received?

The answer would depend on how closely we are able to project ourself to the requirements of the job advertised. Hence highlighting our suitability for the job becomes the focus of the letter.

Similarly, every letter has to have an objective. A sales promotion letter could have any one of the following as its objectives:

- To procure an order
- To introduce a sample
- To request a demo
- To prompt customers to ask for more details
- To ask customers to call for further negotiations, etc.

The text is not difficult to develop, provided the objective is well identified. In simple words, the **text then becomes all about telling the reader, how you can fulfil the objective.**

Two points need to be remembered at this stage:

1. Nobody likes reading very long letters. Keep your letters as short as possible.
2. No one wants to keep hunting for the real message. Deliver your message clearly and quickly.

What do we expect in return?

It is all about spelling clearly to your reader, what you expect in return. This often comprises the last line of the letter. For example:

- *I look forward to be called for an interview*
- *I hope to receive your order at the earliest, etc.*

It is very important to communicate your expectations to the reader. This keeps the communication clear and avoids ambiguity.

Two things need to be kept in mind at this stage:

1. **BE HONEST**: Don't write anything that is not a fact
2. **BE SINCERE**: Don't claim anything that you can't

Further, there is no right or wrong letter. Besides, everyone has his/her own style of communicating. Identify your style and follow it.

Please remember that as long as you remain respectful and sincere, your letter will be received in the same spirit. You don't need to copy from anyone or anywhere. It's always best to be original.

Practical Level – Letter Writing

We all know the basics of writing a letter. The focus of our discussion here is – how to make our letters more readable and

Who are we writing to? What are we writing for? What do we expect in return?

more effective in communicating our message. We discuss here some tips and some commonly committed mistakes. This should allow you to identify those areas in your letter writing skills where there is scope for improvement.

1. Start with the DATE

In the haste of writing a brilliant letter, many people often forget to mention the date. Please remember, it is very important to date your communications. You could put the date either at the top-right or the top-left corner, as per your preference.

Further, it can be written in any way. However, writing it like '3rd June, 2004' or '3 June 2004' would ensure that everyone would read it the way it is written. Otherwise 3/6/2004 and 6/3/2004, could both represent the same date, depending on the system of notation being used.

2. Sender's Address

Many people face the problem of where they should position their address in the letter.

Now, if you were using a letterhead, in all likelihood it would have your address printed. But, in case you were writing on plane paper, you could put your address on the top right corner or at the bottom, just below where you sign.

It is advisable to provide your address and other contact details. This adds authenticity to your communication, and shows that you are serious about what you are writing.

3. Addressee's Name and Address

The addressee's name and address should always come on the top.

Further, almost every communication originating from an organisation would contain a letter number. In case you are writing on behalf of some organisation, please follow the norm being followed at your place of work.

It is not necessary to quote letter number when writing in a personal capacity. Nevertheless, for keeping track of multiple or a series of communications, you could use any numbering system of your choice.

4. Subject and Reference

These two headings allow the readers to know instantly the context of the letter even without reading it.

- **Subject** is about what you are writing in the letter, while
- **Reference** is the link to the previous/pending communication

For Example:

- Sub: Job Application – Project Engineer
- Ref: Advertisement No. 12345

OR

- Sub: Price Quotation – Sample Order
- Ref: Your Letter No. 12345 dtd. 26th June, 2004

You could use either or even both, depending on the requirement. However, do not use long sentences for these two headings. Ideally, they should not exceed a few words as shown in the two examples.

Mentioning subject and reference separately serves another purpose. It helps in keeping the actual text of the letter short and precise. It allows the writer to come directly to the objective, rather than continuing to explain as to what the letter is all about.

5. *Opening Greeting/Salutation*

At the outset, no need to use, for example, 'Respected Mr Dayal'.

'Dear Mr Dayal' would be equally respectable and readily acceptable. Similarly, 'Dear Dr Dayal', 'Dear Prof Dayal' and 'Dear Ms Dayal', etc. are all respectful and acceptable.

Still, if you were not sure how to address the person, which can happen quite often when writing to someone very senior, 'Dear Madam/Sir', would do very well. It is the safest and the best form of salutation.

6. Writing the Text

Do not repeat what you might have already mentioned under the Subject and/or Reference headings. Start writing, keeping the objective of the letter in mind.

Continuing with the examples of Job Application and Sales Promotion Letters, quoted earlier, our letters could begin like,

Example 1:

Sub: Job Application – Project Engineer

Ref: Advertisement No. 12345

Dear Madam/Sir

I have been working for the last 5 years with XYZ Construction Company, as Site Engineer - Ganga Bridge Project. I have played an instrumental role in timely completion of the above project. My various achievements are listed in the CV enclosed.

I am now looking for a bigger responsibility and feel that the advertised position could be the perfect opportunity for the same.

I am sure you would find my profile matching your requirements and hope to be shortlisted for an interview.

Example 2:

Sub: Price Quotation – Sample Order

Ref: Your Letter No. 12345

dtd. 26 June 2004

Dear Mr Dayal

We can provide you three hundred (300) units of product XYZ at a price of Rs. 100 per unit (Rupees One Hundred only), ex-factory as a sample order.

We look forward to the earliest confirmation of the order.

7. *Language*

Please remember you are not writing to win first prize in some creative letter writing competition. You are simply writing to convey your message to your reader, clearly and effectively. A few points to remember:

- Write simple sentences. Make sure your sentences are grammatically correct.
- Don't write very long sentences. If a sentence is getting too long, break it into two.
- Try writing in the Active Voice and opt for active verbs (refer to any High School Grammar book to know more about these grammatical points).
- Use personal references; words like I, we, you, your, my and our, etc. This helps in making the writing look like a face-to-face communication, and thus more acceptable.
- Avoid using lengthy phrases.
- Avoid jargon.
- Use technical terms only if you are sure that your reader would understand them.
- Avoid abbreviations. If used, please provide the full forms as well.

8. *Using Humour*

Follow the thumb rule:

- Official business is serious business, so keep the communication serious, precise and to the point.

There will be several other opportunities in your daily life to display wit and make people laugh!

9. *Vocabulary*

The rule is simple:

- Use what you know
- Use what you are comfortable with
- Use what you think would be comfortable for your reader

It's all between you and your reader. In case you feel the reader is too high profile and well qualified for you to match, then please remember that even such people understand simple vocabulary! So, don't be afraid to use it.

Don't borrow vocabulary from somewhere just to impress someone. Such impressions normally don't last long.

10. Closing Salutation

There was a time, when it was common practice to close one's letter with the remark – *'Your most humble, obedient, servant...'* before signing one's name.

I am sure no one would like to close the letter that way now. Some of the commonly used closing salutations are:

- Sincerely yours
- Yours faithfully
- Warm regards
- Best regards, etc.

You could use any one of these according to your choice, convenience and custom. In some cases you could even simply sign your name.

Anyway, whatever you choose to do, please remember, don't try to decorate this part of your letter unnecessarily. Keep it simple and straight and all will work out well.

This brings us to the end of our discussion on Letter Writing. I am sure the tips discussed above will definitely help you improve the quality of your written communication. To summarise in three points what we have discussed:

1. Be Precise
2. Be Correct
3. Be Original

These three would ensure that your letter is always received in good spirit. The rest is simply practice and how you grow as you learn.

I leave you with this letter, which I have written specially for you, my readers.

26 June 2004

The Reader
Managing Communication
A book from Rupa & Co.

Sub: E-mail
Ref: Chapter No. 2 of this book

Dear Madam/Sir

In our next chapter, we discuss some interesting tips for using E-mail as an effective mode of business/formal communication. So, please keep reading.

Sincerely Yours

The Author
Managing Communication
A book from Rupa & Co.

*

E-mail

*

EVERY NEW thing takes some time to find its roots in society, and only when it is firmly established can the norms and rules relating to its usage start to emerge.

E-mail as a mode of formal written communication has been gathering wide acceptance, and its popularity has grown tremendously over the last ten years.

When compared to a letter, it is a lot more informal in its appeal, relatively easier to draft, quicker to deliver, and simpler to store. All organisations, whether large or small, have started using e-mail as an effective tool of business communication, and its use is likely to only increase in the future. In this chapter, we will talk about some tips that would help you manage your formal/ business communication using e-mails more effectively.

To begin with, the basics of writing formal/official e-mail remain the same both at the conceptual as well as the practical levels as discussed in the previous chapter for writing formal letters.

Nevertheless, since the medium of presentation and delivery is dissimilar, there are certain obvious differences. We talk about these differences in a small list of Do's and Don'ts – ten elementary tips that are easy to remember and simple to implement. So, let's get going.

1. Some Basics

- **Date**: There is no need to write the date or time in an e-mail. The system picks it up by default and displays it automatically, as programmed.
- **Addressee**: The same mail can be sent simultaneously to many people. All we need is to insert as many e-mail ids in the 'TO' column.
- **Subject**: This column should not be empty. Further, it should be relevant to the text of the mail. It should be short and to the point. Something quite similar to the Subject/Reference title in a formal letter.
- **Opening Salutation**: The general rule for the opening salutations is the same as for the letter. Otherwise in an organisational set-up, go by the general norm. Some organisations follow the culture of not writing anything for the opening salutation, starting the e-mail directly with the text. While some others prescribe using informal salutations like 'Hello', 'Hi!', etc. Whatever the case, go by the organisational norm and practice.
- **Closing Salutation**: You could very well store a standard format in your e-mail software that would appear by default every time you choose to write a mail. Otherwise, do as you would for any normal letter.

2. Marking CCs

CC stands for carbon copies. In the past, when a letter needed to be sent to people in addition to the addressee, carbon copies of the letter used to be taken out for the purpose.

Taking out a carbon copy was a tedious job, and the quality of the print deteriorated heavily beyond the third or the fourth copy. With photocopy machines, one could bring out as many copies as one needed; but making copies and then sending them consumes both time and money.

But e-mail can be sent simultaneously to any number of people. Thus a CC can be marked to as many number of people as you wish, without any extra cost, time or deterioration in quality.

This is a big facility, compared to how it used to be in the past. However, every facility must be used properly. Unfortunately, many people and organisations today use it rather recklessly and more frequently than it actually is needed.

Marking CC indiscriminately often leads to communication chaos, specially if a few people to whom the mail might have been sent just for information choose to act upon it or, even worse, forward it to others with their comments.

These are not imaginary situations but real life problems, which are being faced at workplaces across the globe.

Please note that a CC is marked for two purposes:

1. **For information** to a superior or some relevant authority
2. **For some intended action** on part of a third party

It is important to send the mail to the people concerned only. Marking CCs indiscriminately is not at all a healthy habit, and definitely a misuse of the facility.

3. Decorating the Text

A coloured mail, with text in bold and/or capital received from the boss, means the boss is on fire and some bad news in waiting!

However, a coloured mail, with text in bold and/or capital received from a colleague or a co-worker means a tussle for superiority in waiting!

It is not advisable to use colours, bold font, upper case font, underlining, etc. too frequently. These features should only be used to highlight the important points, occasionally.

Using too much of these decorations mostly dilute the value of the message, and it is seldom received in good spirits by the addressee, even if the sender might be the boss.

Your communication should be such that when you send a message decorated even a bit, your readers should instantly know that it's something really important and severely urgent.

Also do not incorporate flashy backgrounds or wallpapers in your mail. These things not only increase the load on the network, but also distract the reader from focusing on the real message.

4. Replying to the Mail

Suppose, you have received a mail from your boss relating to a work order asking you to finish some scheduled maintenance work. The subject of the mail is: 'Work Order No. 12345'.

You go into the field and complete the work. Now you have to inform your boss that the work has been completed successfully. In this case there is no need to start a new mail. Instead, you should reply on the same mail, using the option 'reply to author'.

Here, besides writing in the text the details of the work completed, you could also modify the subject of the mail to:

'Work Order No. 12345 – COMPLETED'

This would let your boss know instantly the immediate purpose of your mail, even without reading the text.

So the rule is: **For continued work, reply on the same mail.**

Let's consider another scenario. Suppose, while you were carrying out the maintenance work at the site you notice another problem, and now you wish to seek permission from your boss for carrying out the repairs.

In this case, you should not use the previous mail. Instead, you should start a new mail. Add a relevant subject line, say something like: 'New Problem – Request Work Order', etc.

Thus the rule becomes: **For a new work, start a new mail.**

E-mail is a very smart mode of communication provided you use it smartly!

5. Adding Attachments

We all know what e-mail attachments are. Just two things about using them:

- Please send only relevant documents as attachments. Don't load your mails and the network unnecessarily.
- Please make sure that the files you attach are clean of any bug or virus.

6. Urgent Action Mails

In most of the modern day e-mail software there are various options to prioritise your mails, and they all can be executed just with a click of the mouse.

The result is that some people simply form the habit of marking every mail they send as URGENT. Please make sure that you don't fall into this habit.

Use this facility only when needed. Also discourage others, if you find them using it too frequently.

Similarly, there might be other types of demarcations. Use them aptly and appropriately to derive maximum benefit out of them.

Don't make your addressees devalue the importance of your communication. It would happen very quickly, if every mail sent by you is marked as urgent and important.

7. Multicasts

In an institutional environment, mails, like those containing circulars, announcements, memos, newsletters, which need to be sent to a larger group of people should be centrally controlled.

E-mail is a very smart mode of communication, provided you use it smartly!

Besides, if a large amount of information needs to be communicated, then the same should be sent either as an attachment or a hyperlink, with only a small executive summary as the text of the actual mail. This helps the readers get the gist of the document and also the choice to read it in detail at their convenience.

In official settings, unless you have been authorised, you should resist from issuing multicasts. A similar criterion can also be adopted for personal mails, as well. Please remember, people do not like receiving or replying to mass-mails.

8. Managing Spam

We all suffer from the problem of Spam. Now there are some tools like Spam Busters that can be useful in managing the unwanted mails; but the best way of avoiding Spam is by not distributing your e-mail address indiscriminately over the web or otherwise. Remember, 'Prevention is always better than cure'.

9. Managing your Folders

It is just like keeping your desk clean, by properly filing all the documents in relevant files and folders and storing them adequately for any future reference/use. Simultaneously, throwing out the useless or outdated documents and keeping all the filing cabinets lean, clean and tidy.

Believe it, finding a document on the computer might sometime become even more tedious than finding it in a filing cabinet, especially if you have to transact through a heavy traffic of mails.

If you feel that the 'Search' or 'Find' options in your computer would rescue you on all such occasions, then happy wishful thinking!

Actually, there's nothing wrong with your thinking; it's just that you have chosen to learn the hard way. So enjoy your dream, as long as it's not broken!

Anyway, it's always better to keep your mailbox clean and well-managed. Arrange your mails as per your convenience in specific folders. Keep cleaning your folders at regular intervals. Use options like 'Archive' or 'Save to Disk' for mails that need to be kept for record purpose.

10. Using Multiple Accounts

Some people, if handling multiple responsibilities, often use different e-mail ids for different purposes. I am not sure how helpful this method eventually works out to be, but it is just another way of managing the heavy flow of information through this mode of communication. You could try its effectiveness for managing your own online communication needs.

This brings us to the end of our discussion on managing communication using e-mails. Remember: **E-mail is a very smart mode of communication, provided you use it smartly!**

At present we are not doing anything on the other emerging modes of written communication, like online chatting and SMS. However the way *thngs r luk'g, v sure wud hav 2 add a chap or 2 in nxt* edition!

Anyway, we would see to that when the time comes. Here I would like to share with you this wonderful story, told to me by one of my teachers, depicting the power of written communication.

An Atheist wrote in BOLD LETTERS:
GOD IS NOWHERE

A Believer came and made it:
GOD IS NOW, HERE

Remember, such is the power of written words. Learn it, use it, and respect it.

*

Reading

*

SO FAR we talked about delivering written communications. Now we will discuss about receiving and interpreting written communication through reading.

Reading is something, which we all do as a matter of routine. Interestingly, all kinds of readings we do can be clubbed into following five categories.

- **Habitual Reading** – Newspaper, Books, Magazines, etc.
- **Unavoidable Reading** – Mails, Letters, Circulars, etc.
- **Essential Reading** – Official Documents (hard and soft), Course Books, etc.
- **Occasional Reading** – Novels, Comics, Story Books, etc.
- **Accidental Reading** – Billboards, Banners, Posters, Calendars, etc.

With so much to read, the question we face is – What should we read? and How much information is sufficient for us?

In this chapter, we will discuss some simple tips that would help you manage your reading habits in a more effective way, and allow you to derive the most out of what you choose to read.

Our discussion will be centred on following three questions:

1. What should I read?
2. What should be the source?
3. Where to find the time?

Subsequently, we will talk a little about some ways of retaining relevant information and discarding redundant information. Let's begin.

What should I read?

- My cousin, who is preparing for Civil Services Examination, reads almost everything that might come his way. He reads three newspapers in a day, two current affairs magazines in a week, books on subjects relevant, and his notes prepared over the years.
- My friend, who is a doctor, and waiting for his super specialisation, reads books and journals on the area of his specialisation. He also surfs the web for relevant material, goes through the notes and summaries of various conferences and seminars, and studies the case histories of the patients in his hospital. In his free time, he loves to read romantic novels and watches television for the news broadcast.
- My colleague, who heads the sales team, does not believe in reading too much. He is a man of action. However, no

pamphlet, poster, booklet, banner or document relating to our industry, passes his eyes, unread. He will occasionally glance through some business magazine or go through the internal newsletter, but will not miss reading the comic strips and the cartoon in the newspaper every morning.

- My uncle, a lawyer, finds himself busy reading two things. As my nephew describes them, dirty looking files with damp papers inside and thick boring books with no pictures. Once every week he would read *Ramcharitmanas* for an hour, and being a sports buff, goes through every word on the sports page of the newspaper. Further, being an active member of a social group, he has to read a lot of letters, etc. relating to his work over there.

We all have different requirements, and we all have varied likings and preferences.

- Identify **your requirements** based on your professional/ career objectives
- Gauge **your interests** depending on your personal likings and preferences
- Assess **your needs** based on social, organisational or family obligations

And you will know the answer to the question – What should I read?

What should be the source?

Once a professor of a leading B-School told me that nowadays a large number of submissions made by the students are downloaded from the Internet. He said that he gets to see a lot of copy-paste stuff, unlike the older days when it used to be text hunted out of the books in the library.

Today, information is available to us from a large number of sources. We have to choose the one best suited to our needs and requirements.

- My father subscribes to a professional magazine. He just scans through it to keep himself abreast with the changing trends. Otherwise, it is his routine work that keeps him constantly updated about the developments in the field of his work.
- My father's colleague subscribes to a fortnightly newsletter, which he receives via e-mail for the same purpose. He says he has no time to read anything more, as the official and essential reading would take away all of his time.

There would be numerous sources of similar information. You have to choose the one which you feel suits you best. Please remember – **It's better to read just one document; but it's important to read it well.**

Further, make sure that the source is authentic and provides correct information.

Where to find the time?

Many people struggle to find the time to do the reading work. I have seen it at my place of work that my colleagues, who work mostly in the field, are often unable to even read their routine e-mails for weeks at a time. And when they finally open their mailboxes, there are so many pending mails that there is no way they can read them all. The question is – How do we find time to read?

Interestingly, we always find time to do three types of things:

a. The ones which are of our **interest**
b. The ones which have become a **habit**
c. The ones which are a **compulsion**

If you feel you need time to read something, include it in one of the above three categories and you will find the time for it … anyhow. Believe me and try it out!

Retaining/Discarding Information

We might read a lot, but might not retain as much. Secondly, we might not know what is worth retaining and what we should actually discard!

What should I read? What should be the source?
Where to find the time?

These questions one can learn to answer only with experience and time. However, what we must always do is develop a formal mechanism of storing information/knowledge for future reference/use.

For example:

- We could use a simple diary for noting down the relevant points
- We could generate a computer database or a power-point presentation
- We could draw a chart for new information
- We could develop a file for pasting the relevant clippings, etc.

These measures are of course in addition to retaining things in the mind. For authors like me, it is very important to store relevant details, as we don't know, when and where we would need what!

So anything that sounds interesting, finds a place somewhere in our record keeping set-up. Simultaneously, we also keep discarding material which is no longer relevant. This power of discriminating between relevant and redundant information comes with experience only – there cannot be any hard and fast rules.

Thus you have to learn by making your own mistakes; and mistakes you will make only when you make a beginning!

SECTION B
VERBAL COMMUNICATION

*

Public Speaking

*

ADDRESSING A LARGE audience from the stage – this very simple looking task, ironically, sends a chill down the spine of countless number of people.

A friend once told me, that in a survey in the United States, it was found that the fear of public speaking was only next to the fear of death!

I don't know how true it is, but yes, dry mouth, wet palms, shaking hands, shivering knees, thumping heartbeat, sweating foreheads are not at all uncommon to public speakers, both experts as well as novices.

In this chapter, we shall learn the secrets of effective public speaking and ways to countering public speaking related anxieties. Our discussion will focus on the following areas:

- Stage Fright
- Writing the Script
- Captivating the Audience
- Length of Speech
- Keeping things Relaxed
- Speaking Extempore
- Managing Interactive Sessions

Stage Fright

As a child, Winston Churchill would go into the woods and speak aloud to the trees, to get over his fear of public speaking. This is what my Hindi teacher had told me when I was in Class VII and was preparing for my first debate competition.

Later, she asked me to practice speaking aloud facing a blank wall. 'Imagine that you are addressing a huge gathering sitting beyond this wall,' she would tell me.

This training was highly effective, and I gained in confidence for my speech by following this simple technique.

Just a day before D-Day, I asked her that although I was confident to deliver the speech forcefully, as she had advised, I was still a little afraid of facing my friends, classmates and teachers. 'What happens if one of my classmates teases me by making a funny face, or just starts laughing at me?' I agonised.

'You don't need to look at any one of them,' she had said, adding, 'Keep your face towards the audience, but focus your attention on an imaginary line, just above the head of the audience in the last row. Keep moving your head from left to right and back, slowly over this imaginary line. This will make everyone feel that you are speaking while looking at them, when actually you would be looking at none of them.'

Bingo! The trick worked perfectly and fetched me the first prize. Even though my knees had kept shaking all through the speech, my voice was firm and face relaxed and that is what mattered.

I still use both these techniques, i.e. speaking to the wall for practising my presentations and looking into nowhere while speaking, whenever I feel uncomfortable while delivering a speech.

It is not that only beginners who face stage fright but sometimes experts also do. The only difference is that the beginners buckle under the pressure and panic, while the experts find some quick solution and carry on with the show.

Actually, we don't fear the stage. What we fear is the reaction of our audience! Anyway, whatever be the reason, two things can help us get over this fear:

1. **Prior practice** (like speaking to the wall or to the trees or to a dummy audience)
2. **Ignoring the audience's presence** (like looking at the imaginary line or into nowhere)

As you gain in confidence as a speaker, you will automatically start facing your audience more directly and start speaking looking into their eyes. It's not at all difficult. It's simply all about practice.

And don't worry, if the legs are shaking or palms are getting wet or the heartbeat is running faster. You are not the only one who would be experiencing all this. It happens with everyone.

The more confident a man looks on the stage, the more shrunken he might be from the inside. So why worry about something that is so rampant. Just carry on with your speech and everything will turn out to be perfectly fine.

Writing the Script

It is important to decide beforehand what you are going to say. At the outset you must know the subject. The better you know the subject, the more confident you will feel writing the speech and subsequently delivering it.

The text of the speech will depend on two things:

1. What is the topic?
2. Who is the audience?

People, who know too much about a subject, often find it difficult to restrict their speech to the domains of the actual topic, and also within the limits of understanding of the audience.

You might know a lot about the subject, but your topic might not require you to deliver all. Besides, your audience might not be ready to accept all. A good speaker would always adjust to the level of the audience, rather than making the audience come up to him.

There is another issue relating to writing the speech.

Many people can write and memorise their speeches with ease. However, there are a few for whom this task is slightly difficult. I have always struggled to remember my speeches, but that does not mean I don't plan them.

On most occasions, instead of writing the entire text, I write down the important points on a piece of paper or on a small card. I carry this card with me and keep referring to it, while speaking.

On some other occasions, I simply make a mental note of all the points. I don't carry any cards and just speak from my memory, recalling one point at a time.

It is actually all about practice. If you are a beginner, write your speeches beforehand, memorise them and deliver them. As you grow in confidence, you could start using other techniques as well.

Captivating the Audience

While delivering the speech, any speaker would know instantly how his/her speech is progressing. The reaction would come from the audience. If your speech was actually hitting the imagination of your audience, you would find them sitting observant and listening to you eagerly. Otherwise ... you simply would know!

Every speaker wants to captivate his/her audience. But what is the secret? We discuss some simple tips that would help you hold the attention of your audience, while addressing a gathering.

1. **Don't read; instead speak.** Reading is self-indulgent, while speaking is participative. Your audience will appreciate you more when you address them directly. Nevertheless, that does not stop you from referring to your notes occasionally.
2. **Look at them while speaking.** You are there to address the audience. If you are afraid to look at them directly, at least create an illusion that you are looking at them, as discussed earlier in the chapter.
3. **Stand firm and relaxed.** Don't bank too heavily on the podium or on the table, etc. Also don't move too much across the stage. You can use your hands, your facial expressions and your body to make a point, but don't move them too much. Remember, you are not performing a dance but delivering a speech. At the same time, you are not in the parade ground either. So don't stand soldier-stiff. Be relaxed and at ease, as if talking to a gathering of family members or friends and discussing some very serious issue.
4. **Talk Business.** Eventually, what you speak is what will actually matter. Thus make sure that your speech is clearly written and properly drafted. Further, the background of the subject should be clear in your mind, otherwise you would never be able to deliver it with clarity and conviction.

Give them what they want and you will get what you want, and that's the real secret of successful public speaking!

5. **Speak Clearly.** Your voice should be clear and audible. Neither too loud, nor too slow. When in doubt, please check with your audience. If they can hear you clearly, it's fine; otherwise, make necessary adjustments. Please don't hesitate to ask for confirmation.

The Length of Speech

Many people, once they start, don't know how to stop. While others, simply don't know how to start!

A subject which is familiar and of our interest can make us speak for hours at length. At the same time, an unfamiliar subject or a difficult topic can make us run for the nearest shelter.

There is always a big dilemma. How long should the speech be?

The rule is simple: As long as it is intended. A good speaker will always respect the time allotted to him. He will neither wrap up half way nor continue speaking forever. He will deliver the message keeping in mind the time provided.

It basically comes with practice. Once you discipline yourself to the limits of time, you automatically learn the ways to extend or curtail your speech and still deliver the message.

Also, keep in mind that it is difficult to hold the attention of your audience, if you are delivering too much or for too long. People usually do not have very long attention spans.

A good speaker will only deliver as much, as would be absorbed easily by the audience. Hence knowing the audience is very important.

Keeping Things Relaxed

A lot of people deliver their speeches with great art. They tell stories, include doses of humour and still keep the audience captivated. If you are wondering how they do it, the answer is – it all comes with experience.

It is just like driving. When we learn driving, initially we are always tense on the road. In those times, even a simple obstruction or traffic jam can make us nervous. However, as we gain in experience, we become relaxed and are able to drive without bothering about so many things. We are able to manoeuvre the vehicle through the thickest of traffic and the roughest of roads.

Secondly, as for humour, it is something very serious. It's very difficult to make people laugh. In using humour in your speech, you have to be very sure that it would work in the right spirit and in the right direction. Otherwise, the results could be devastating. There is no problem in using humour during the speech; but use it with discretion, and keeping the overall purpose of the speech in mind.

The beginners should avoid using jokes, etc. in their speech. They should stick to the core objective of the speech. You can always make things light by incorporating examples, stories, case studies, etc., which are accepted more readily by the audience and are also easier to deliver than jokes.

Speaking Extempore

On several occasions, we don't get time to prepare an elaborate script. We just have to speak extempore. It could be for an extempore debate competition or making an announcement in the school assembly or while addressing your subordinates and workers at office.

There are occasions, when we are simply asked to come up and address a gathering. How do we handle such situations?

The basic rules remain the same as they are for a formal well-prepared speech, except that you have to speak from memory. On such occasions, quickly jot down a few points on a piece of paper, if time permits; or make a mental note of points you would like to address.

Use simple language, and just ensure that every sentence you speak forms a natural link with the one coming ahead.

Speaking extempore is basically a game of mental strength and confidence. There is no need to keep speaking for too long. Deliver the core message and come out quick.

Managing Interactive Sessions

What are the interactive sessions where public speaking skills are of great significance?

- Teaching in the class
- Being a Quiz Master
- Compering a Panel Discussion
- Conducting a Seminar
- Hosting a Talk Show, etc.

These are some of the activities that are interactive in nature, and where our public speaking skills are constantly tested.

The most important challenge for the person conducting an interactive session is to keep things moving on track. When a lot of people start speaking at the same time, there are chances that things might get chaotic and go out of hand.

Like it happens in a class, where the teacher does not exercise sufficient control over the students; or at the talk show on the television, where the host allows too many people to jump into the discussion at the same time.

Managing such sessions is an art, which can only be mastered with real practice. It can in no way be taught through a book or in the class. You have to learn it, while on the job. I suggest, start by managing a class and then move upwards.

Please remember, managing interactive sessions is all about keeping your audience informed about the fact that you are the master of the show, and you are the one who calls the shot. The rest will simply come with experience.

And finally...

Some of the most interesting and captivating public speakers of our country have been our politicians. It would be demeaning the entire effort if I don't mention at least a word about them in this chapter on public speaking. So here's a story of a Netaji.

The Netaji was getting ready to leave for an election rally. He called his newly appointed secretary and asked him to bring the copy of his speech.

The Netaji read a small portion of the speech, and said in an agitated tone: 'This is not my speech! Where is my speech? Bring it immediately.'

The secretary got a little confused: 'But Sir, this is your speech. I have written it just now.'

'You fool, what are you trying to teach me?' By now the Netaji was furious. 'Go and bring my old speech.'

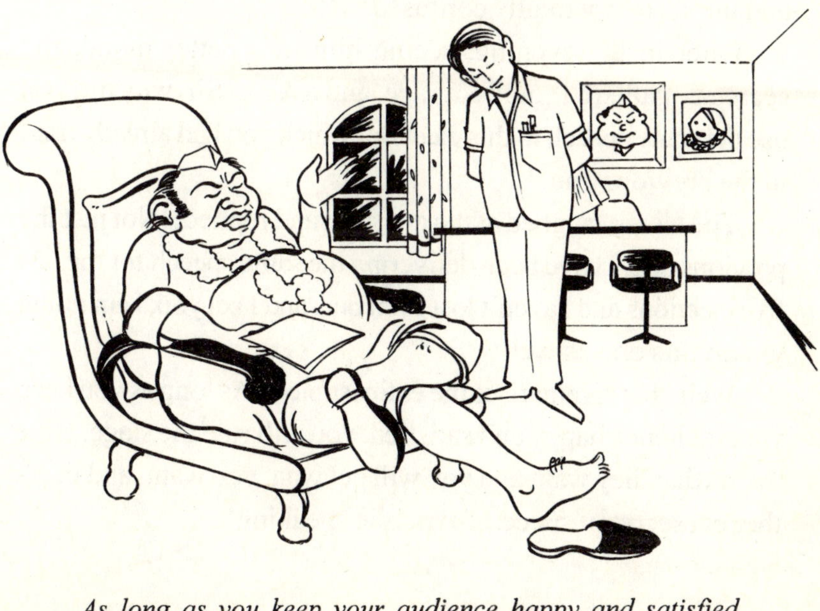

As long as you keep your audience happy and satisfied, you will rule the stage.

The secretary, who was a well-educated intelligent young fellow, could not understand why the Netaji wanted the same old speech, which he had used during the previous elections. However, seeing his boss in anger and with no other job in his pocket, he didn't dare to argue and quietly brought the speech.

The Netaji took the speech and went to attend the rally. Interestingly, the rally turned out to be a big success and his speech was greatly applauded. The Netaji was extremely happy and the secretary totally confused.

Later in the evening, seeing him in a better mood, the secretary gathered some courage, and asked, 'Sir, why did you use the same speech in this election, which you had already used in the previous one?'

The Netaji laughed at the question and replied, 'Not just the previous one. I have been delivering the same speech for the last five elections and haven't lost even one, and I bet you, I am going to win this one as well!'

Well, this summarises the entire subject. As long as you keep your audience happy and satisfied, you will rule the stage. Give them what they want and you will get what you want, and that's the real secret of successful public speaking!

*

Business Presentations

*

MAKING PRESENTATIONS for business and official purposes has become an essential feature of today's working life. Even students are often required to make such presentations for their projects, etc.

In this chapter, we shall discuss some essentials for delivering effective presentations using slide shows. Specifically, we will discuss:

- How long should a slide show be?
- How much should be written on a slide?
- Is it appropriate to read from the slide?
- How to make the presentation interesting?

However, before we begin our discussion, it would be interesting to recall this famous story from the court of the great Moghul Emperor Akbar. This is one of the famous Akbar-Birbal stories.

Once Akbar became furious with Birbal over some issue and asked him to go out of the range of his sight. Birbal had no option but to follow, and thus went away to some unknown place.

Time passed, and soon Emperor Akbar started missing Birbal, his wisdom and his witty humour in the court. The emperor started regretting his decision and ordered that Birbal be called back to the court immediately.

Messengers went in all directions to look for Birbal, but none could find him anywhere in the entire kingdom or outside. Now the emperor was in a fix on how to find Birbal?

The emperor thought for a few days. He knew he would have to do something extraordinary to get Birbal back, and hence decided to hold a contest.

He announced that whosoever would demonstrate to him successfully that he can be half in the sun and half in the shade at the same time, would be entitled to a huge reward.

The courtiers did not understand the purpose of the crazy sounding contest, but none had the courage to speak against the wishes of the emperor. So they quietly got into the job of making the contest a big success.

For the first few weeks, some people came and gave demonstrations to prove their suitability for the reward, but none could convince the emperor and were rejected.

Akbar was extremely confident that only someone like Birbal could win. However, as the weeks passed and no one turned up with a convincing display, even the emperor started losing hope of finding Birbal again.

Then one day, while the court was in progress, the gatekeeper came in and told the emperor that a man, who had come from a far-away village to see the emperor, claimed that he was half in the sun and half in the shade.

The emperor ran towards the balcony to have a look. Down below, he found a villager standing in the middle of the lawn, with a charpoy on his head.

In that state, he was indeed half drenched in the sun with the light filtering through the gaps between the charpoy strings, and simultaneously half covered in shade with the shadow of the strings forming on his body.

The presentation could not have been any better, and the emperor knew instantly that his objective had been met.

The most important thing about a presentation is that it should deliver the message in a demonstrative manner. It is about taking your audience as close as possible to the real-life experience.

For example, if you were making a presentation to impart training for using some new equipment, your sessions would be effective only if you incorporate a live demonstration of using the equipment.

It would become even more useful if you make your trainees try their hands on the equipment, thereafter. This would take them closest to the real-life experience, and give them the necessary confidence to use the equipment in the course of their work.

Incidentally, if your mind is still stuck on the question whether the emperor eventually succeeded in finding Birbal, then the answer is yes. Further, if you wish to know how, I suggest you pick up any one of the readily available books on Akbar-Birbal stories to learn the answer.

The most important thing about a presentation is that it should deliver the message in a demonstrative manner.

For the moment, we shall discuss the essential points of delivering an effective objective-oriented presentation.

Managing Slide Show Presentations

Slide shows are not something unknown to us. We all know what they are. Making presentations using slides is a very common practice these days. The term 'slide', which we are using here, would include presentations using:

- Charts and Diagrams
- Transparencies
- Photographic Slides
- Video on Television
- Computer generated slides
- And even live models/equipment/instruments

Of all these methods, handwritten or typed transparencies are used most widely for academic purposes, while computer-aided presentations are used for business purposes.

Please note, all our public speaking skills will come handy while delivering a presentation. However, there are certain issues specific to slide show presentations that we shall discuss here.

How long should a slide show be?

It would depend on the objective of the presentation. However, any show of more than 10 to 12 slides (about 45 minutes to 1 hour), becomes highly challenging for the presenter in terms of holding audience attention.

For longer presentations, it is advised to incorporate sufficient breaks in between; or making presentations interactive enough to keep the audience alive.

How much should be written on a slide?

Some presenters have the habit of crowding their slides with too much information. Please remember, slides are not books or even letters. The idea behind using slides is to allow the audience to grasp the message using her/his eyes and ears. It is just another aid to help you deliver your message more clearly.

As a thumb rule, deliver your headings through the slides, while adding audio descriptions using your own words.

Heavily crowded slides make the readers confused. They try to read what's written, simultaneously trying to listen what you might be saying, creating confusion, distraction and disillusionment.

Is it appropriate to read from the slide?

Are you there to do a book-reading session? No, you are making a presentation. So, don't read from the slide. Instead, speak while guiding your audience through the slide.

People, who write too much in their slides, often end up reading from them. The others who read from their slides are the ones who come without doing any homework ahead of their presentation.

How to make the presentation interesting?

Some Tips:

- **Distribute a printed copy.** If possible, you could distribute a printed copy of your slides to your audience before delivering the presentation. This helps making things a little interactive. The audience feels better involved and thus is more participative.
- **Use handouts/models.** In case it is not possible to distribute a copy of the slides to everybody, you could always distribute a few handouts, some diagrams, statistics, graphs, tests, exercises, games, etc. to be discussed with your audience. You could also arrange for some simulation exercises involving your audience. All these things are especially effective for presentations of longer duration and/or with a larger gathering.
- **Keep things participative/interactive.** The success of a presentation depends on how interactive it is. By its very nature, a presentation has to be interactive/participative. It is not a monologue from the speaker to his audience, nor is it an open-house discussion or a meeting where anyone can speak anytime. It is perhaps in between the two. The presenter has to invite his audience to participate and still has to keep the things under control.

It is about taking your audience as close as possible to the real-life experience.

For the rest, it all comes with practice and experience. Once again, there is a limit to what can be taught through a book. Using the guidelines provided here get into the real thing, and thereafter, improve as you learn. And don't forget Birbal, who delivered the perfect presentation by sending a man with the charpoy on his head, thereby also enabling the emperor to find him!

*

Meetings, Interviews and Negotiations

*

AS THE title suggests, in this chapter we have clubbed three topics of neighbouring interest.

I

Meetings

Many people call meetings a collective waste of time, and in many ways they actually are. Still, a good part of our working life goes into meetings, and some of them are essential specifically for aligning inter-personal communication within an organisation or a group.

As individuals we can participate in a meeting in two capacities:

1. As an organiser
2. As a participant

We shall discuss both the scenarios separately.

Being an Organiser

The organiser holds the principal responsibility for the productive and desired outcome of any meeting. The points that one must keep in mind are:

1. **Decide the objective** – Why is the meeting being called? What possible outcomes do you expect from the meeting? You should be clear about them.
2. **Work out the agenda** – How you plan to achieve this objective? Points over which discussion shall be held and decisions taken. Mark them out.
3. **Invite the participants** – Please don't invite everyone; rather just the people who would actually matter in discussing the whole agenda. If need be, have a one-to-one meeting with the person concerned. Make sure that people are aware of the objectives and agenda before they come for the meeting.
4. **Controlling the meeting** – The meeting should be objective oriented. It is the responsibility of the chair to keep things on track and ensure that the agenda is strictly followed.
5. **Speaking to the chair** – Make sure that all communication in the meeting takes place only through the chair (Chairman/ Controller of the meeting). No one speaks without the permission of the chair, and no one addresses anyone else but the chair. No brickbatting among the participants.

Meetings are essential specifically for aligning inter-personal communication within an organisation or a group.

Being a Participant

Remember these five points:

1. Listen
2. Don't speak unless you are asked to speak
3. Speak only what is relevant to the agenda, and speak to the chair

4. Don't brickbat or try bullying the colleagues
5. Stay objective and follow the proceedings

For the rest, if the snacks being served are not of your liking or the coffee is too sweet, you can leave as soon as the official stuff is over!

II

Interviews

Interviews are a very common mode of communication. We could be a part of it as an interviewee as well as an interviewer. We shall discuss both the scenarios briefly. Please note we are restricting our discussion to the selection interviews only. We are not discussing other types of interviews like media interviews, etc.

Being an Interviewee

Actually, my own experience over the years as an interviewee makes me completely confused when it comes to writing about the subject.

I am saying this because whenever I thought I have had a wonderful interview, the results said otherwise. And at places where I had no hopes or had gone for the interview only reluctantly, I have almost always been selected.

However, that does not stop me from remembering this wonderful experience which one of my super seniors had while appearing for his Civil Services interview.

It happened that as he walked into the room, his foot got caught in the torn carpet and as a result he lost his balance and fell on his face.

(How many of you can dream of such a dream start!)

As he got up and gathered himself, the chairman of the Board remarked,

'Well, you seem to have fallen at the very first step!'

'Yes sir, and what a great fortune to have fallen in such an august company,' replied the interviewee beaming widely, and the entire board burst into laughter.

So next time when you go for an interview, just remember these three things:

1. Keep your cool
2. Be yourself
3. Enjoy the show

The rest perhaps only God knows; so leave that on Him.

Being an Interviewer

Taking an interview is an even bigger challenge. I don't think there is any way you can select or reject anyone by talking to him/

Keep your cool; Be yourself; Enjoy the show.

her for five or ten minutes, asking a few questions based on what's written in his/her CV.

Anyway, if the job falls on you, you have to do it. So, keep three things in mind:

1. Give them a proper chance to prove their suitability
2. Ask questions that would highlight their usefulness
3. Go by your gut feeling when making the selection

Give them a proper chance to prove their suitability;
Ask questions that would highlight their usefulness;
Go by your gut feeling when making the selection.

For the rest, there are better and bigger experts to advice and provide guidance on the subject, and I would suggest you to seek their counsel for more information.

III

Negotiations

A very important part of a meeting or an interview could be performing negotiations. There are times when situations reach a deadlock. On such occasions, we always wonder how to negotiate to make things move forward.

Before we talk about some tips to negotiate successfully, three points need to be kept in mind regarding negotiations.

- At the outset, a negotiation can take place only when both (or even all) the sides concerned are willing to lose some ground in order to gain somewhere else.
- Secondly, a negotiation can be successful only when it makes things as close as possible to a win-win proposition. No negotiation would last if it results in a win-lose or a lose-win scenario.
- Thirdly, not all issues are negotiable. Negotiations can take place only up to a limit, after which they become worthless and one has to take a firm stand over the situation.

For example, in the *Mahabharata,* the Pandavas sent Krishna to the Kauravas as their ambassador, because their objective was to give peace a chance, even at the cost of losing their kingdom. They asked for only five villages; but since the

Kauravas were not willing to yield even that much, the negotiation process broke down and the war was announced.

A negotiation can take place only when both the sides concerned are willing to lose some ground in order to gain somewhere else.

However, as long as you are on the negotiation table, you could follow some of the following tips:

The Initial Analysis

- Identify what is causing the deadlock
- Ask yourself – Can it be solved?
- Ask yourself – Am I willing to bend?
- If yes, how much or to what extent
- Identify the motives and reasons for the present behaviour of the opposite side
- Are you being played win-lose!
- Does the opposite party respect your interest or are they indifferent?

The Process

- Offer an initial escape route, a compromise formula, etc.
- Explore needs and priorities
- Identify new linkages and trade-offs
- Introduce fresh entry points
- Use relationship as variable
- Listen Actively
- Plug the loopholes to make things come as close as possible to a win-win situation

The Safeguards

- Let your opposition know that you are not prepared to be pushed around

- Use emotions positively
- Remember nothing you do is 100% logical
- Pay heed to your instincts

I would repeat once again that a successful negotiation can happen only when both the parties are willing to find an amicable solution. This would mean, each leaving some ground for the other.

Negotiation is a two-way process and can never be unidirectional. Your efforts should be to try your best to come to a common ground. However, if you feel that things are getting unidirectional, remember, you should always retain the option of taking a decision.

And Before We Close...

I can close this chapter as well as the book here. I have said what I had to say; but don't you think it would be like making an exit on a very serious note? I feel this interesting story will be a more appropriate conclusion to this chapter, as well as this book.

There was a small school in a small town far-off. One day, the Inspector of Schools came there for a surprise inspection and directly entered a class. He told the teacher present that he would like to ask the students a few questions.

The teacher nodded in affirmation, and the inspector indicated towards a student sitting near the window towards the back of the class, to get up and answer his question.

'How much is five plus five?'

'Eight,' answered the student in an extremely confident voice. Even before the inspector could say anything, the teacher intervened and said in an applauding tone:

'Very good! Now sit down.'

No one can develop anyone.
A person has to develop on her/his own.

All the boys clapped and the inspector was surprised. He asked the teacher, 'Don't you know how much is five plus five?'

'Of course Sir, I know,' said the teacher.

The inspector was further surprised. 'Then why did you applaud the boy's wrong answer?'

'Sir, until two days back this boy had been answering "six" for the same question. Now you have to give him time to come to ten,' said the teacher with a smile.

No one can develop anyone. A person has to develop on his own. Others can only support the process. Hence, anything you might want to learn, you will have to learn on your own. The path is simple, get up and get into action and the lessons will start coming automatically.